KINDRED

KINDRED

A Family Portrait

Illustrated by Sam Rusztyn

Monica E. Smith

iUniverse, Inc.
New York Bloomington

Kindred

A Family Portrait

iUniverse books may be ordered through booksellers or by contacting:

iUniverse
1663 Liberty Drive
Bloomington, IN 47403
www.iuniverse.com
1-800-Authors (1-800-288-4677)

ISBN: 978-1-4401-0429-9 (pbk)
ISBN: 978-1-4401-0430-5 (ebk)

Printed in the United States of America

iUniverse rev. date: 10/30/08

ALSO BY MONICA E. SMITH

Days of Fine Gray Ash

Available from blurb.com

Going Coastal
Dog-matized: The Comical Truth of Life with a Jack-A-Bee

This Book is for My Children

Diverse and lovely
They color my days
And brighten my life
With a thousand suns' rays

God in His kindness
Allowed them to bloom
The flowers in the garden
Of this mother's womb

and

Dedicated to those
who have found
in nature
a kindred spirit

Contents

TO EVERYTHING ITS SEASON

THE SIMPLE PLEASURES OF NATURE

PREFACE

Our connection with nature is a strong one. Henry David Thoreau felt that we can never have enough of nature. I agree! We take comfort in her coolness, warm ourselves in the heat of her sun, are awed by her beauty and amazed and frightened by her power and anger; and we respect her wisdom. What person has not longed to "get away from it all" when life's pressures become too demanding? And what are our first thoughts in the search to escape life's burdens: to the woods, the lake, the beach, the mountains and the sea—to nature! It's like coming home.

In his book, *My First Summer in the Sierra* (1911), John Muir states "We are now in the mountains and they are in us, kindling enthusiasm, making every nerve quiver, filling every pore and cell of us. Our flesh-and-bone tabernacle seems transparent as glass to the beauty about us, as if truly an inseparable part of it, thrilling with the air and trees, streams and rocks, in the waves of sun—a part of all nature...". I never felt this so much as on a recent trip to Yosemite National Park with my family. To simply stand in the midst of giant Sequoias as they swayed, cross streams and rivers of icy cold rushing water, climb the mountainous rock-laden paths and sit in the warmth of the sun was all I needed to feel alive, to understand who I am. People spoke in hushed tones and acted with reverence, and I became aware of the ever-increasing feeling that I was in a sacred place, the song of bird and wind and waterfall all in perfect harmony, perceived as psalms to the Creator.

Taking this even further, the German physicist, philosopher, G. C. Lichtenberg once said "we cannot remember too often that when we observe nature, and especially the ordering of nature, it is always ourselves alone we are observing". I visualize this as looking into a mirror. And that, my dear friends, is the seed from which this book was born. I believe this with all my heart: that there is but one Architect of the entire natural world. And I believe that from the earth we came, and when we complete our time in this world, it is to the earth we will return, for we are kindred…

Morris E. Smith

Photo by Scott F. Smith (Yosemite National Park)

GRATEFUL ACKNOWLEDGMENT TO THE FOLLOWING PUBLICATIONS/WEB SITES FOR PREVIOUSLY PUBLISHING MY WORK

(any error or exclusion of publication is purely unintended)

"And Let the Rain Fall Down"—*Quill & Parchment*, March 2005

"Beauty and the Beast"—*M.A.G.*, Summer 2003

"Chasing Coyotes"—The Other Voices International Poetry Project, Spring 2006

"Chill"—Skyline Literary Magazine, 2002

"Fog"—*Penney-A-Liner*, Summer 1996

"January Rain"—Tamafyhr Mountain Poetry, Issue #42, 2006

"Never Say Never"—*Dufus*, Issue #11 2005

"Oh, To Be a Noble Tree"—Poetic Voices, August 1999

"Reawakening"—*Poetry Life & Times*, March 2004

(published under the title "Transmutation")

"Rivulets"—The Other Voices International Project, Spring 2006

Shadow Poetry Anthology (*Shadows of the Season*), Winter 2004

CREAM, the Creative Medium, October 2003

"Solstice"—*The Eclipse*, August 2000

"Summer's Return"—*ESC!*, Fall 2005

"The Case for Coyotes—*Carnelian*, April 2005

"The Moon Resplendent"—*Lucid Moon*, August 2001

"True Colors" —Skyline Publications/A Hudson View, 2002

"(Un)like the Bird"—CREAM, the Creative Medium, February 2003

"Wind"—*Ibbetson Street Press*, December 2000

"Winter"—*Skyline*, Winter 2004

OUR KINSHIP WITH NATURE

When one tugs at a single thing in Nature, he finds it attached to the rest of the world.

John Muir (1838-1914)
naturalist, writer, and conservationist

Oh, To Be a Noble Tree

Oh, to be a noble tree
And never have to bend a knee
In the bonds of slavery
Or know the pain of poverty

Regarded as a thing of beauty
Lovely for the eye to see
Not concerned with vanity
Each accepted as he would be

Oh, to be a noble tree
Akin to sun and stars and sea
No fear of inequality
For such a royal pedigree

With difference each one's majesty
And color, just variety
To live a life forever free
Oh, to be a noble tree

So Cold the Winter

so cold the winter
so cold
the hearts of some
afraid
the ice will melt

so cold are some
so frightened
to offer love
cautious
of giving too much

so protected are they
so sad
the hearts of some
safe
and empty without love

(Un)like the Bird

I fritter away my days
Setting lofty goals
I believe I cannot accomplish
A bird, twittering
In the treetops
But, unlike the bird
Which takes wing
On flights of fancy
In a moment's notice,
I am grounded
By my own uncertainty

Solstice

Joshua prayed to the lord, and said...Stand still, O sun...O moon...
And the sun stood still, and the moon stayed...(Joshua 10:12-13)

A solitary leaf clings to a barren tree
even as I try to hold on to my youth

and like Joshua of old, I pray for the sun
to stand still in the sky, the moon to cease its orbit
if only for one day,

that I might slow the assailing seasons
and hold at bay the ravages of time

Chasing Coyotes

Captivated by their cunning,
We chased two coyotes
Down the back roads
Laughing like children
In the pseudo-safety
Of her convertible.

"There! There they are!"
I gasped, searching frantically
For my camera.
But they had disappeared

Much like her childhood.
And, like her childhood
I wanted this moment
To last forever.

Wouldn't you know it,
The coyotes took off
Down another road,
And ours dead-ended.

Kindling

I am an ember warmed by love
Taking comfort in the heat, enkindled
By only one spark from its passion
Given life only through its consummation

The Moon Resplendent

The moon, resplendent in crystalline halo,
rises reverently over an open field
singing a silent hymn to its creator.

As I sleep, my soul chants in harmony
with the lunar oblation,
awakening me to the oneness of life.

Come morning I arise, radiant in the sun,
rejoicing in my new-found kinship,
nevermore a solitary soul.

Chill

My eyes remain fixed
Upon the newly fallen snow
Its outward beauty notwithstanding
I feel a chill as I gaze upon it,
Remembering a previous encounter
With the frigid whiteness

Some people are like the snow
Their outward beauty notwithstanding,
I must turn away from the glare
I feel a chill when I see them,
Remembering a previous encounter
With their frigid indifference

Passage

Among the fallen
Lay the ancient ones,
Beautiful in death
As they were in life
Petrified, they remain still
Where once they stood tall
Nodding their delight
In the evening breeze
And yet, as in testimony
To resurrection
They shine in splendor,
Vivid and brilliant, gilded
In morning sunlight

Emulation

Nature charms me.
It is that simple.

With her ancient wisdom
both majestic and modest,
she leads me into paradise
that I might know order
and harmony, purity and grace

She forgives feeble attempts
to emulate, knowing
I intend not malice but honor
as I search for the beauty
and innocence within myself

THE POWER OF NATURE

Who has seen the wind?
Neither you nor I:
But when the trees bow down their heads,
The wind is passing by.

Christina Georgina Rossetti (1830-1894),
English Poet

Reason and Rhyme

Where is the reason, the rhyme
in a world that honors force?
Look to the wind.

in a world that glorifies might?
Look to the mountains.

in a world that praises power?
Look to the sea.

in a world still seeking beauty?
Look to the flowers of the field.

in a world struggling to be free?
Look to the birds of the air.

Where is the reason, the rhyme
in a world desperately in need of love?
Seek God within yourself.

Beauty and the Beast
(variations on a theme)

BEAUTY

hoary limbs
(once rough and notched)
become sleek and smooth
and without imperfection
born anew of freezing rain
the newly-formed crystalline boughs
dance and shimmer in the moonlight—
nature bejeweled by nature

* * *

THE BEAST

the merciless cold rain
hurls its icy daggers
parting limb from tree
(and I from thee)
once alive and fruitful
the pain of separation
is now realized—
nature deprived by nature

Wind

blows where it will
and waits
for no one.

I sometimes wish
I were the wind…

January Rain

Isn't it funny
How a January rain
Can bring about a downpour
Of tears, how the cold, somber
Sky brings to mind the passing
Of years?

Gone, again,
The tranquil glow
Of holiday candles,
The warmth of heart,
The pure feathery softness
Of a Christmas Eve snow.

Out with the old, in with the new
We chant, one and all
Cheering last year's passing
While we welcome the unknown,
When it is the unknown we truly fear,
The past we hold dear.

Isn't it funny
How a January rain
Can bring about a downpour
Of tears, how the cold, somber
Sky brings to mind the passing
Of years?

Jazz Fest (Columbus, Ohio Riverfront 1997)

The jazz rang sweet
Till it lost its beat
When driving rains came
And took their aim
Made the water run deep
As the skies began to weep
While strong winds blew
Hail pelted and flew
And the thunder did crash
As did lightning flash
The trees bowed and swayed
With people who prayed
Until the sun heard
And gave the word
Caused the fury to cease
And the torrent to ease
Soon the people cheered
They no longer feared
Now the jazz rang sweet
Never skipped another beat

Season of My Discontent

These bleak, damp days
Clamp down on me

A steel-cold vise
They strangle,
Choking out each emotion
As if simply feeling
Was an impediment to being

Where is the sun rising
To lift this grip of sadness?
Where is its shawl
Of penetrating warmth
That would enfold me,
And melt a heart frozen
In the lowering gray
Dawn of winter?

Beyond the Grave

In truth
If I were blind,
My sight peeled away
As the rind of some bitter fruit,
I would still know the dawn
I would still feel the wind.
Never stifled by the leanness
Of my senses
The dawn would still glow,
The wind blow;
For nature is immortal
And exists beyond the grave.

NATURE'S GIFTS AND OFFERINGS

Wherefore did Nature pour her bounties forth
With such a full and unwithdrawing hand,
Covering the earth with odours, fruits, flocks,
Thronging the seas with spawn unnumerable,
But all to please and sate the curious taste?

John Milton (1608-1674) *Comus* (l. 710)
English poet, scholar, writer and patriot

Oblation

Fog rises

Incense hovering
Mystically over valleys

Enveloping
The highest peaks
And treetops
In a heavenly haze

Nature's sacramental
Offering
To her Creator

Her Nature

Her nature is not ours.
Her beauty simple, upright
Transcends us all
Making the heart throb
At mere sight of her.

She arranges in her hair
Fragrant ribbons
Of variegated velvet,
She warms us
With her golden smile
At daylight
And perfumes
Our moonlit midnights
With soothing scents
To calm the restlessness within

By no sweat of her brow,
Without the slightest hesitation,
She discloses more of her secrets
Anew each day—
Purely for our delight.

Twilight

and the moon rose and the sky
spread its coverlet of neon colors
before me, a feast for my eyes

and the stars were aglow
with a wild light, dispelling
the approaching darkness of night

no gift was more revered than this
image, this divine masterpiece
sent for my beguilement

and speaking with all due deference,
I addressed the Giver in low tones,
reveling in the transcendent offering

Sanguine Expectation

He waited, imagining
In breathless anticipation
As each silken layer
Was slowly,
Almost painfully
Peeled away
To reveal
The delicate gift
Flowering within.
As if to sense
He could take no more,
The tiny green bud
Finally, mercifully burst
Into a profusion of color

Spring had sprung!

Through Death, Life…

Consecration

A solitary leaf, lovely in death
as it was in life, glistens
in an argentine shroud

It flutters in a late autumn breeze
to its frost-covered resting place
on the gelid ground below

Is it aware its interment
is self-sacrifice,
that winter might again
draw its bitter breath?

* * *

Reawakening

'Tis a slow death for some,
the color lingering almost resentfully,
gradually paling in the oblique winter sunlight
desperately clinging to life

Finally, autumn's last leaf is set adrift
upon a sudden gust of arctic air
and freezes, interred in the gelid ground
with which it melds to become
the blood of new life

Who?

Each night he arrives
Outside my bedroom window,
This preening troubadour
Who serenades me
With his ballad
Trying to win my heart.
Who-who-who
Who-who he croons,
Each night the same old song.
But before I can lay eyes on him,
Whoosh!
And he is gone.

Summer's Return

Fall's fluorescent foliage
Burst forth in brilliant hue
In the ashen light
Of an early morning sun,
A not-so-subtle foreshadowing
Of winter's fated fury

Summer's days were numbered
And, gracefully, she bowed
To the radiant array of fall's display.
She would return one day
In the heat of passion
To embrace her world—
Once again

Come October

Copper and gold, these riches I treasure
More than any earthly pleasure
Come October they shimmer in fields of grain
A harvest of color, in nature they reign
Behold their beauty, store the memory, look fast
But the blink of an eye and the season has passed

IMAGININGS

It is the marriage of the soul with Nature that makes the intellect fruitful, and gives birth to imagination.

Henry David Thoreau (1817-1862)

Face of an Angel

I oftentimes gaze into and beyond
The glazed iridescence of an intricate sky,
Following with my eyes the spiraling clouds—
Those shallow shoals of heaven's amaranthine shores—
I am filled with unheralded emotion as I wonder,
"Might I be looking into the face of an angel?"

Cloudscape

At thirty-five-thousand feet
Over Minneapolis
The clouds appear thick, splayed

A plush carpet laid before the feet
Of a mythological king or, perhaps
Cushioning the throne room of a god

I cannot help imagining how it might feel
To walk barefoot through the feathery
White wisps and I chuckle to myself,
Almost feeling the velvety fluff
Tickling my toes

Night Sounds

The raging wind and rain
seem almost musical to me
as they break and swell, break and swell
in perfect harmony.

At night the sound seems magnified
as it echoes through my mind,
and causes strange imaginings
not unlike a glass of wine!

Excitement wells within me
as I perceive this curious sound.
It strikes a chord of fantasy
seldom ever found.

A little while longer then
and sleep will take its hold,
while the sound escapes to distant shores
and in memory unfold.

Never Say Never

The ice storm was all-consuming,
young and old alike ripped limb from limb,
dried and drained of life, encased within
icy chrysalides which caused each tree to sway
and bow and plead for mercy

My heart first fell with a thud
from a wailing winter wind and I feared,
certain as I knew the unicorn existed only in fantasy,
that nothing of beauty could arise
from these cold ashes of devastation

Yet, from the corner of my eye shone a gem,
a sapphire sparkling in the night;
turning toward the light in awe, I saw
it was not a gem at all, simply an ice-blue branch
radiant in the moonbeams

But for one brief, unshakable moment,
I believed in unicorns

Rebirth

The sun sank slowly
into an ashen sky
as if to stall
the day's good-bye,
and, thereby, spawning
rosy hue as pledge
to return
and shine anew

Fog

In the darkness of night it crept in silence,
embracing each thing with a gentle mist

Softly, its hazy shadow
was cast upon the hard-frozen earth,
creating an image of complete peace

I delighted in the ethereal beauty
and was acutely aware of the hush
that had fallen with the fog, muting
the starkness, the harshness
of sight and sound,
transforming each object by its presence—
for one brief moment

Telegraphy

What a terrible sacrifice, seemingly,
This transition from summer to autumn,
And cruel in the way it is believed
Our dying to be cruel.

But if you could see beyond
The physical, see beyond
Human perception, perhaps
You could envision the connection
Between life and death, understand
That they are two halves
Of the same whole, perhaps

You could imagine the invisible
Transmission between seed and root
And twig, as if the telegraphing
Of a message of life, not death,
To slow the heartbeat, not stop it,
That the tree might scatter
Its seed far and wide.

The Case for Coyotes

It doesn't frighten me,
their far-off yowling,
more a plaintive cry
than the howl
of a vicious animal,
almost a consolation.
I hear their nightly lamentation
seeming to denounce civilization
where there is killing without cause,
and I am curiously comforted.

True Colors

Virgin snow sparkled
in the winter moonlight
bold white

Like purest diamond shards
it shone throughout the
cold night

Would it seem as pure
come morning's softer
gold light?

Reverie

In the early evening,
When the sun takes on
A bright, crayon-red splendor,
The world becomes bathed
In shades of scarlet casting
An eerie glow across the sky.
Birds, flying quickly by, seeking
Suitable sleeping quarters mimic
Their delicate counterparts, artfully
Constructed origami creations
Caught up in a swift night breeze.
Puffy clouds become turtles
Overjoyed to be above the rain,
Not needing to duck their heads
Into radiant rounded shells
(Amusing mosaics of the reflected
Hues of evening.)
Look up! Lose yourself
In the fairy tale kingdom
Of an evening sky.
Look up, and indulge in reverie.

TO EVERYTHING ITS SEASON

Nature gives to every time and season some beauties of its own; and from morning to night, as from the cradle to the grave, is but a succession of changes so gentle and easy that we can scarcely mark their progress.

Charles Dickens (1812-1870)

Transfiguration

In the passing seasons is seen
The ever-changing, ever-growing
Cycle of our lives

The infant spring gives way
To the heated passion of youth—
That summer we think will never end

But as certain as autumn is to follow,
So too adulthood and the cooling
Of youthful desire

The winter wind wails and moans
Without warning,
And beneath its mournful cry
Echoes *too soon, too soon*

But the unending cycle brings again
The promise of spring
Winter's death is but a passing
Into the realm of the spirit

Where we, transfigured
Don a new garment, to die…
Nevermore

Family Tree

Autumn arrived before
I was prepared, before
I was aware
It would be so cold

And my children, falling leaves
Caught up in a whirlwind swirl
Away from our family tree
(Away from me)

I look toward the horizon,
See the coming snow
And I can only pray
The winter will be mild

Life Cycle

The autumn beauty fades too fast
As into winter it must pass
And winter, too, must know its bounds
For spring demands to make its rounds
The summer sun, its time bemoans
When fall becomes its chaperone
To each the time is precious, dear
For soon will come another year

Silent March

Though she may arrive silently,
Lamb-like, March cannot hide;
Her bright red pails handily hung
Give her away,

Announcing her arrival
With the pomp and ceremony
Of a royal entourage, signaling
time for mapling once again

March, sweetest of months—
Syrup flowing into our midst—
Allows us to savor life's fullness

God's Ear

The wind blows far
Beyond my window
It carries new green seedlings
(Longings, needs, dreams)
Tossed hither and yon

Higher, ever higher they ascend
In a whirlwind of faith and hope
Until they are planted
At just the right moment—
In God's ear

Turn Turn Turn

She is exposed.

The last of her finery
Released by a cold snap,
Leaves bestrewn
By a winter-born breeze
Lurking in icy shadows

Paying homage, she bows
Fairly kneeling before
The approaching winter solstice,
And flushed with seeming defeat
Begins to weep

For she knows
Her restoration lies
In the transient spring

And Then There Were None

She is fourth of four, gone now
To find who she is meant to be
And with her, I fear, my purpose.
But she has found hers
As they each have before her,
One by one by one.

Had I read the small print
So long ago, the sadness
I now carry within my heart
Would still not be diminished,
Nor would the sun be forced to rise
Above this stone-cold steel-gray dawn.

Yet, I must rise above it
That my life might radiate outward
Reflecting meaning once again.
For this is the rituality of nature,
Its flow and matter of course—
Is it not?

Rivulets

Our days
belong
to the clock
dictated
by incessant
chiming
Each new hour
nudges us
onward
ever onward
never
allowing us
to linger
in the moment
Rivulets,
all of us
surging
until
we drift
with the
shoal water
into
eternity

Lady Luna

She would not pass this way,
would not grace my eyes
with her rubicund silhouette
for many years hence;
for she had been eclipsed,
and willingly took her place
in the order of nature,
This luminous creature,
the queen of the night
outshone by lesser stars.
And so I shall moon away the time
until she comes again in her glory,
to shed her fulgent beauty.

Where Once a Lowland Corn Field Stood

There is a shallow filmy pool
Where crops could not survive,
Where once a lowland cornfield stood
And languished, never thrived

'Twas washed away what could not flower
But the land was not left barren,
Where once a lowland cornfield stood,
I now behold the heron

It is said that nature runs its course
And life is born of death,
Where once a lowland cornfield stood,
Another now draws breath.

Life is sustained through nature's wisdom,
Change its only order,
Where once a lowland cornfield stood,
Snowy egret now is boarder

THE SIMPLE PLEASURES OF NATURE

The best remedy for those who are afraid, lonely or unhappy is to go outside, somewhere where they can be quiet, alone with the heavens, Nature and God. Because only then does one feel that all is as it should be and that God wishes to see people happy, amidst the simple beauty of Nature...

Anne Frank (1929-1945),
German-Jewish refugee/diarist.
The Diary of a Young Girl (1947; TR. 1952),
Entry for Feb. 23, 1944

Simple Pleasures

Give me a sapphire sky above my head
With stars to guide my way
An alabaster moonlit night
And the golden sun by day

Give me trees to teach of beauty and strength
Flowers in every hue
The rain to quench my thirst for life
For temperance, the morning dew

Give me wind at my back to ease my way
A breeze to cool desire
A gentle breath that whispers love
And for passion, give me fire

Give me the soft green grass throughout my life
On which my feet may tread
But when this body breathes no more
Lay me down in earthen bed

Woodsmoke

Silver smoke spiraled
around a blackened chimney
and faded into a frosty mist.
The smell lingered long
after the woodsmoke vanished
deep into the cold winter night.

Her Majesty

In the midst of her evergreen entourage
Stood the Maple
Majestic, brilliant, glowing as if ablaze
Yet not consumed by her radiance
Nor could October's hoarfrost
Cool the intensity of such perfection
And I, how blessed
To have gazed upon such royal pedigree

She Loves to Watch the Trees

She loves to watch
The trees sway and bend
As they whisper their love songs
To autumn's brisk wind

Though lightning might threaten
And thunder impend
Or if rains on high
Begin to descend

No matter if sunlight
Should come to an end,
How she loves to watch
The trees sway and bend

Winter

Some believe
winter is cold and lonely
harsh and devoid of life
(they feel only the sharpness of wind
cutting through them like a knife)
They cannot feel
the warming sun
that melts the driven snow
offering new life to tender roots
as it trickles far below

Some believe
winter is desolate
with nights mournfully dark
(but they see only with their eyes)
I feel with my heart
The stinging warmth
of a winter wind or the snow,
though it may inter
no, never have I felt so alive
as in the dead of winter

Mesa Verde Monet

Out here clouds mimic
The mesas, using the sun's
Kaleidoscopic spectrum
As their palette.
It is difficult to tell
Where cloud leaves off
And crag begins, each one
A shining intuitive creation
Framed between the canyons
In a masterful sundown display.

Solemn Song

Early mourning, break of dawn
I hear them sing their solemn song.

Side by side, wing to wing
Perched high in the old ash tree,
They sing.

Oh, the enchantment!
How can there be
Such beauty in sadness?
'Tis a mystery to me.

Well-to-Do

My wealth lies
in the splendor of nature, for
she adorns the modesty of my life
with her abundant riches:
The shimmering crystal
of winter, the lingering
fragrance of spring,
the golden times
and palmy days of summer,
brilliant-hued autumn leaves
hanging as a tapestry upon the trees.
In these I am very rich indeed,
for herein lies not only my wealth,
but my joy and sufficiency

I Want (To See …To Feel … To Live)

I want to see the sun rise and set
and rise again
I want to feel its warmth penetrate my soul,
the coolness of my skin as daylight dies away

I want to see the muted hues of morning
delicately caress each silent, shadowy form
and watch them finally fade
into paleness, into blackness
as they take their leave upon the day's repose

I want to awaken with the first light,
experiencing each new moment
as with eyes that have yet to see
I want to rest peacefully at the time of completion
regretting nothing, knowing I had truly lived

And Let the Rain Fall Down (Prayer)

While I live
Let the earth come
To know me as her own.
Let the sun bestow
His warm embrace,
The wind gently caress
My world-weary face,
And let the rain fall down
To bless me.

But when I die
Let the earth receive
Me as her own.
Let the sun avert
His radiant face,
The wind guide my soul
To a higher place,
And let the rain fall down
To bless me.

ABOUT THE AUTHOR
(and Author Comments)

 Monica Ellen Smith began writing in 1991 at the age of 40. Intrigued by the rhythm and "sufficiency" in the brevity of poetry, she was inspired to give writing a try, soon created a web site dedicated to writing and continues to write poetry to this day. Her inspirations have been Robert Frost and Mary Oliver (for their love of nature), Pablo Neruda (for his passion), William Carlos Williams (for his simplicity) and contemporary poets Nikki Giovanni and James Kavanaugh, among others.

Monica also greatly enjoys the poetry of Jenny Joseph, especially the poem "Warning" (the "Purple Poem"); she had written a poem in response to "Warning" which she sent to Ms. Joseph, who was "amused and flattered" to know that her poem had been the inspiration and catalyst for Monica's creativity.

She enjoys writing about everyday things, and feels that a poem can be found anywhere. Her family continues to play a most important part in her writing. They have always had confidence in her, even when she wasn't so sure of herself. Family and friends have been the subjects of much of her better poetry, as "Love makes for a fertile garden in which poetry can grow".

About her writing, Monica explains "I enjoy writing accessible poetry, and feel poetry need not be written in a complicated language for the select few. I find, even in the brevity of poetry the freedom of expression, and in that there is freedom in expression." She feels what is most important after the writing of a poem is the sharing. The two must go hand-in-hand, as it is the sharing/experience of the poem which makes it live. "Many times, people experience the same feelings but do not know how or are unable to express them. To see that the poet has felt or experienced what they have provides a precious link with another, giving a sense of belonging."

Monica believes that interpretation most definitely has its place, but has all too often been misused and abused. "I believe that poetry should allow for symbolism but it is not necessary. Sometimes less really is more, simplicity being the rule. A perfect example of this is Robert Frost's "Stopping by Woods on a Snowy Evening". There is a story that Mr. Frost had been hounded to death about the "real meaning" of this poem, so much so that at one point he had said "I've been more bothered with that one than anybody has ever been with any poem in just pressing it with more than it should be pressed for. It means enough without being pressed." He went on to say that the only thing the poem means is "It's all very nice here, but I must be getting home. There are chores to do." Another time, when being pressed by a critic who believed the last three lines implied that Frost longed for the after-life of heaven, Mr. Frost simply shook his head saying "No, it only means I want to get the hell out of there."

Monica is the author of *Days of Fine Gray Ash* (a collection of poems regarding the many nuances of love, which was endorsed by Poet/Author Nikki Giovanni), available through her web site. She has also authored two books available at the http://blurb.com bookstore: *Going Coastal* (photography) and *Dog-matized: The Comical Truth of Life with a Jack-A-*Bee. Her poems have been published in many national and international journals including *Carnelian*, *The Muse Apprentice Guild* (M.A.G.), *The Fairfield Review*, *The Taj Mahal Review* and *The Other Voices International Project* (invitation only). Some of her work has been accepted into works dedicated solely to charitable endeavors.

Most recently, she has had poems purchased for two of author June Cotner's books: *To Have and to Hold: Prayers for Newlyweds* and *Miracles of Motherhood: Prayers and Poems for a New Mother*, both of which where released in spring 2007. Another of her poems is being kept by Ms. Cotner for a future book. Monica also has had several poems included in many of the PoetWorks Press anthologies, the latest of which—*Baby Boomer Birthright*— was released in October 2008.

Monica enjoys reading and exploring her family ancestry, as well as her new-found love of photography, which she calls "silent poetry". She has been experimenting with creating Haiku-Photography, a form which has recently risen from the original Haiga (Haiku Painting). Two of her Haiku-Photography poems were published in the February 2008 issue of *Sketchbook— A Journal for Eastern and Western Short Forms.*

Monica was born in Cleveland, Ohio and now resides in West Liberty, Ohio with her husband, Scott and Beagle/Jack Russell mix, Bernie. They have four grown children: Jeremy, Aaron, Nathanael and Veronica, who are pursuing careers throughout the United States, giving Monica and her husband "rent-free accommodations" as they explore the country.

ABOUT THE ILLUSTRATOR

Sam Rusztyn has always had a passion for art, and animation. An artist, painter, and animator by trade, Sam has recently graduated Sheridan College with a B.A.A. in Animation. A love of all creatures, especially dogs, horses and spiders helped create an award winning film for the last year of school. In the future, Sam hopes to continue making films, illustrating books, and is currently working full time for an animation company in Canada.

www.ingramcontent.com/pod-product-compliance
Lightning Source LLC
Chambersburg PA
CBHW031303280526
45784CB00004B/1964